To everyone that stuck around

<u>The first few symptoms</u>

So at this point in my prophecy, whose archer will I
be?

Cause in which stage the foreshadow would come in,

As whatever I lay my eyes on a blank canvas is all I
see,

Should i wait or let my elegy eulogise me

Mirror mirror on the wall

Even if they tried, I wouldn't be best

so much they tried, all they let go

Did whatever in their might to keep me afloat,

Now all those versions of me lie dead as they go.

<u>Cameos</u>

How come I regret every step I take

All those flashbacks kept me awake

They always say I have it in me

with a thousand questions

running cause at this brink of reality,

it's their preoccupied haze I partake in

~~Roll~~ the credits

Like the end of a movie I've seen

I lived never as the main character

But always as the third lead,

Who lurked in the corner

Would do everything to keep her image clean

Just to be given a minute of spotlight

Starchild, they called her,

But that minute's over now

She's still in the spotlight, though

As an example of wasted potential

A "what to be not"

Starchild

No one ever made me into a perfect, cynical clone

In the end, all I became was the wasteful potential I
had never shown

I never was good enough, and I never let go

So how can I grieve someone I never knew

The Star

<u>The corpse (ft. The alchemist)</u>

For the first time, all eyes on me

I'm the magician

Whose tricks all went wrong

Surrounded by scenes of calamitous lamentation,

Acts of generalised reciprocity became disguised by
deep altruism

18 years later proudly they stand with my Achille's
heel in hand

While hating on me was the only time they escaped
their labyrinth and ran

I
THE MAGICIAN

<u>The most beloved daughter</u>

I'll see you when the spirit meets the gone

And no traces of reciprocity are shown when I'm
sitting all alone

And every cynical clone ought to get me

I think they forget that I'm not one of their own

And they'll sit at my grave to claim I was sane as I lay
blood struck inside

They'll use all my diaries on the bookshelf to prove it
how I deserved it,

how it was a hoax I perpetrated on myself

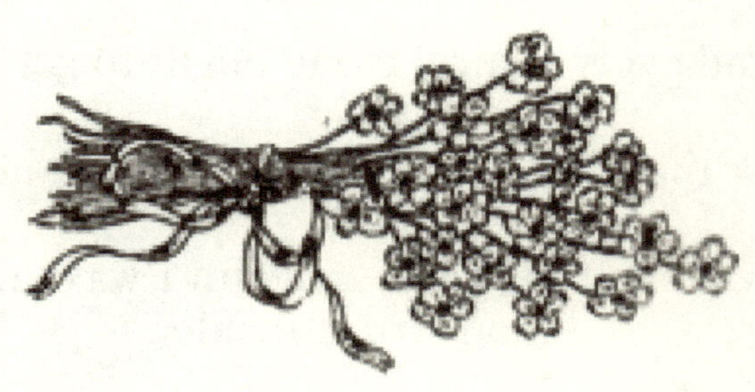

The greatest victim mindset

I always wanted to know how I lived in moments
that I stole

Still always in the supporting role

I always had to beg and borrow time, but now I've
crossed the line

And took away the shine,

although they were never even mine

It's the last stage in my prophecy

As I lie here covered in illiteracy

Irony became the central theme in the story of my
life

Came this far,

scheming my way like a criminal

Looked for other ivies through every road I took

And sang of melancholic lies as truth became a
peripheral archive

The forgotten history department

Even the forgotten history department forgot my existence

But you wouldn't,

won't you ?

Won't you sit beside me and tell me it's all fine?

Cause all those barbed wires weren't mine alone

Won't you ask me to come home while I lay six feet deep?

But I promise to collect all the stars that have your spark in them

I'm sorry if I ever leave you alone in this mayhem

Wannabe romantics

Wewere dressed to the nines

The mysticity of the situation made me think you were mine

January 12 I never wish to forget

They say stars align, but my entire universe did that night

I'll pray to every single god that surrounds me

If that means crossing paths with me becomes something you never regret

Hope this doesn't end up being obsolete

Can't you see I'm willing to ruin myself for you on repeat

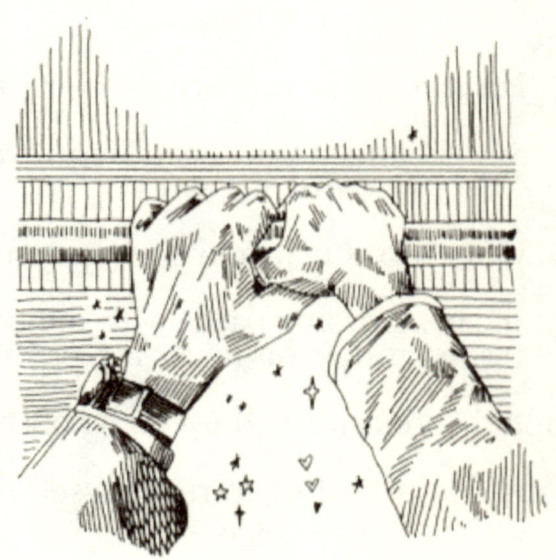

A very visible witch

Can't you see we were written in the stars

Admiring from afar turned into my version of
tranquillity

Its been a year now what started as immortal

Turned into something ephemeral in 8763 hours

But those memories will forever be in me,
imperishable

Liars are those who say put yourself above always

But I'll die for you in these unnamed streets

If that means the invisible string will tie you to me

999
Of Wands

One's very own bereavement

Tip toeing around the hallways that we once called
home

With the blade stuck on my waist,

Watching you watch her with the same eyes

Oh, how deeply altruism runs in your bones

But it's my time to make a move

You always said you'd die for me in secret,

would you though ?

<u>I think she did it</u>

For the first time in the last 33 years,

the sun rose in its full glory.

It's kinda humourous how prettily it glistened on
your blood

88 stabs for 88 times you said you loved her

Look what you turned me into

I ended up becoming my very own nightmare

Now finally, all the stars align,

same as the night we first met

So how farther with this knife could I get

You treated me as if everything was a lie

So that night ended up becoming my forbidden ally

Psychoticism: stage 4

They say to die by your side is such a heavenly way
to die

But I hate you with all my might

I hate the fact you never called, and maybe never
intended to show up

I hate you didn't want me enough to come back

I hate how I try to change everything to just make
myself deserving

In the end, your memories end up being anything
and everything I'll ruin myself for

It's been 3 years now.

I paced around and stumbled upon a gravestone

They said it's time to move on

So I dug up another grave of a name similar to
yours

<u>1+1=2 bodies</u>

Prosecution is what they call it

I was at home that night

I lied

The blade's not mine

I lied

I know I said I won't let you down

But looks like my prophecy came true in the end

Did the foreshadowing come early on

The whispering garden, it says on the board,

I promise it won't be your fault when I'm dead and
gone

The archer's near now

The woods, trees coloured with all of my tied
threads

Never was known for getting ahead

Looks like here, the story of us ends in dreads

The only open door

I'll have all the murals and sad prose

If that means you'll guide me home

But it's too late now the spirt has met the gone

Destiny acted like my potential never shown

The whispering garden turned into my only exile

One's indefinitely another's reality

Legacy of gods surrounds me

Yet I prayed to the wrong one

Cause whatever dies doesn't stay dead

You're alive in my eyes

Fate never led me to your midas touch

Past the cuts and bruise

I lost all there was to loose

The holy roman army died in every duel

I'm alone, so alone

The kingdoms fell, so did the empire

This labyrinth that I created became my only attire

The dead is never wrong

Funny how just one person took you away

investigators said something this brutal would only be
seen on screens

Every brink of my home ended up screaming your name

Whether it be how we laughed together or your blood
stains,

She knows damn well how to cover up a scene

Blood dripping out of your eyes,

It must be exactly how she must've wanted it to be

She knows damn well how to keep her image clean

No one believes me when I saw her leave

Where did she go,

Nobody knows

All hues turned blue in the colour palette of my life

So what took me so long to realise dooms day was near

I was never meant to be her nor could i ever be

The paradoxical haze never been so clear

THE TOWER

<u>Long story short, three died</u>

Master of spin ended up giving us rings

With an underlying promise to never be around

I tried to change the ending, ended up losing everything

Devil all around him saying you get what you reap

So what kind of fate do you want it to be?

I ended up being the one you loved in secret

While saying you'd bleed your soul dry for me,

I guess it's time for me to leave me

Follow the mystical haze and you'll be on death's
disposition

So I went to the whispering garden

and finally found her.

The blackest white magic

Every brink of me is now haunted

With your handprints on my soul

So picture me on these streets

Where they buried me in ignominy

But how you went to her

Became the empire's biggest felony

But destinies are written and forever doesn't last

Always dug the past to avoid us turning into an illicit
affair

Did she set us apart? Did I turn into a distinct period
of your history?

Devil lurked in every line in my book every time you
looked at her

While those lurking glances overshadowed every inch of
my integrity

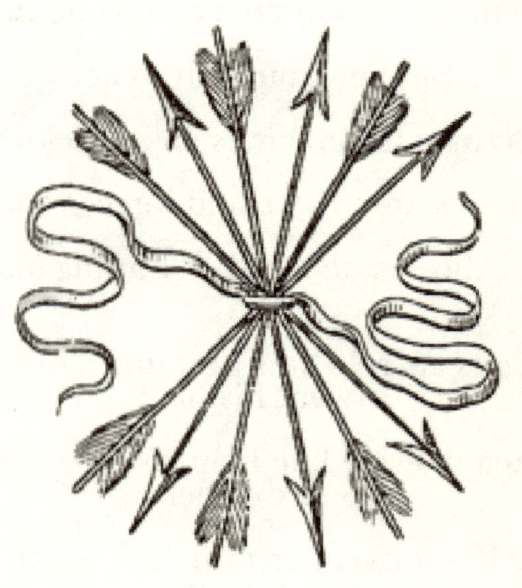

<u>Purpose</u>

I search these unnamed streets for rhymes

Just to be dug back up alive

Just to be stolen away every brink of light

I never knew how to feel,

But just someday I might

Always forgot I wasn't ideal

Yet it felt so alive

But never was real

Just someone you've paid for

I think I forgot how to be an ideal daughter

Something I'm not,

Something I can try to be

It's something I weighed for

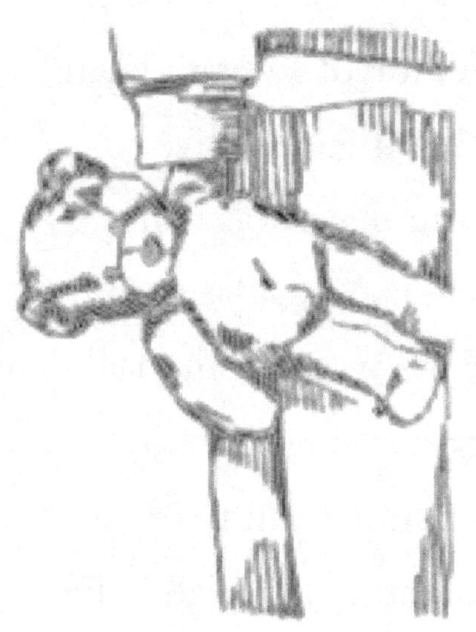

The familiar familial ache

Turns out they like hunting witches too

While I die trying a millionth time for you

And those moments are also few upon which they stroke
their saviour's complex forever,

You were nowhere to be found while they went all
around with their notions

About what happened after that fight

About what happened that night

Didn't have a single clue,

but they spoke with so much conviction

I don't care who believes you or how many afflictions
surround us

Even if the supposed killers hide west, I'll still give you
my best

You get what you reap they said

And you best believe if clarity is in death,

they'll go that far

Cause the truth rests dead with him beneath

Death of a lake

The death of the lake ,

Near the house we grew up up in

Did it keep you awake?

More than the fact that I lay in felony I didn't commit

A year went by

Eventually I got dug back up alive

But you were too ashamed to show up

Even when you were supposed to protect me

Too ashamed to care for my anomalies

Altruism in runs every letter when you say you got a
brother in me

But people like you never bring serenity

Your coverted bravery inflicts in every step you take

Still only the hue of blue, my priority was you

Will you ever offer me stability?

The killer's right judgement

May I ask a question?

Where did you end up going in the middle of the
night?

In the car,

did you fight destiny with all your might?

Only to find out you'd not end up right

And what did you choose?

the aftermath turned into the "saints" making fun of
you

Cause now all of them asking if you were in your right
mind

While they consequently failed to provide

Wanting you dead has really brought them together

May I ask a question?

"The first everything"

They said it, didn't they?

They said you were extraordinary

A prophecy worth writing in the stars

They said fake it till you make it

But you never did even start, did you?

Always talking about when the spirit meets the gone

In the blue hue

But every time you texted him, you killed that little girl
all over again

Leaving all the bystanders, even yourself, confused

While I blamed it on my issues,

And the rumours let loose

In my mind I was your muse

Only ever wanted to be decoded by you

The forgotten history department seems like my new
ephemeral life

His first loml

Cause if we enter that era, would we ever return?

Churn through the pages

Just for two graves to get undone

Although the alchemy of romantasizing you was so fun

Just to find compassion and frustration in each line

Among all the chapters you happened to be "real one"

Cause when the idea of death is in the air, no one can
hit you

Scramble the feelings you had into my issues

It's been a year since I'm at the hospital waiting for you
to come get me

While you preach out there that you really fucking
loved me.

Principles not the situations

All those insults in disguised under love

Weare so similar yet million worlds apart

You peeped in through the creeks of us

For a moment made me realise no one was above

Pressuring me to come through putting me in a state of
astart

Made me feel dented in hopes of love for you

That left me in denial, partially buried

But came back each time,

baby, the way you play is legendary

Not once asked me why my portrait turned out to be
like this

Yet the way you nonchalantly said you loved me was
unnecessary

Distorted my opinion of love, rinsed me with hopes of
bliss

then threw me off the same cliff that,

so momentary

left me alone in the cemetery all disguised under love

Made merealise we're all born poets

Until we kill them one by one

The beloved 15 year old

"Clouds in the sky looked like marshmallows to me"

But I know you don't remember when I said that

Saw me bleeding, yet never looked at the scars,

You let me be

Distorted my opinion on love of my own entity

I adored you so much that my heart couldn't even fit
the adoration in

Now the same sky's covered in blue hues, all resembling
you

I guess all the sins I committed were way too hollow to
lure you in

You've not been able to escape,

nor have I ever since.

<u>It was all us</u>

Did you do it on purpose or was it a lie?

You're so different,

I lie to myself to see you as alive

When he hung himself, did you die too?

While he went to motels

A beginning wasn't there to begin when it comes to us

So busy being a good person,

you sacrificed us in the process

I can't even imagine being in your shoes

Whether it's stripped childhood or calamity in the walls
of your own home,

I tip toed around my life trying to not make a sound

So why do I end up in the middle of the feud?

Don't you realise the two blades always seemed to cut
me through

Now I can't love someone even if I wanted to

what did I do to deserve the hell you gave me

Pretended everything is normal while bureing me
illicitly

But it's getting hard to breathe now

I wanna shove you in the same grave you buried me

Loved you

Even the greatest of great is at a point afraid

Of losing something that cannot be replaced.

Waiting to be guided home

That maybe was never theirs

But in all incongruity, it leads to

The paper moons I once made for you,

that lie in my room

With the stuff I'm willing to throw

I'll happily let my version of you go

While you plead not guilty with blood on your hands,

When does it end?

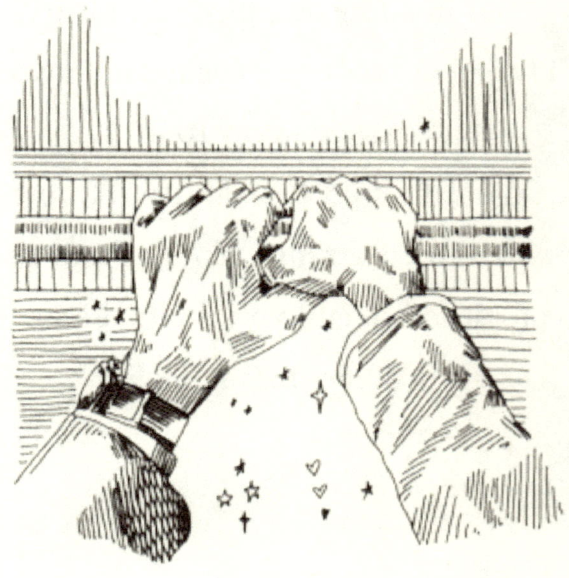

And the clock strikes midnight

To whom do I owe the greatest apology ?

To the person I became or the one I couldn't ?

To the one who got killed ?

Or the one didn't ?

And what if they cross paths

Different lifelines but the same darn clock

False god to false applauses,

One chased the spotlight

The other gave her all

but never really got it right,

Yet they feel so alive, for the first time

with no one to watch

For they cried themselves to sleep

Preaching "nobody gets me"

Yet it felt so right

So why did they end themselves this time ?

They look through the creeks of their childhood home

And it's best believe that no one is home

They turned out to be the most full filled

When stranded all alone

<u>It'll get better</u>

There's a knock on my door

And how my desertion of you wishes you came through

What else can I do except wait

"I would lose myself at this rate,"

While I fell apart, you'd swore by some rules or
principles you once saw on a screen sitting in your room

Taking me for some goddamn fool

And I swore it was a string or fate

And god knows how I hate people banging windows

So, I allowed someone to bang on my door all over
again.

<u>"Accept and be grateful"</u>

There's a video of you in gallery

Did you get enough love ?

In ninety-one days

While I went to hell and above just to feel loved

Why did you lie?

So many subtle promises yet a valiant goodbye

Do you feel loved now ?

With the external validation you've grown on all your
life

Does the kid in you feel cool?

When you talk about those nights with me,

With elaborate lies

To those who give you hope that they'll give you tickets
to the show,

That the kid in you has never known

Dolls have eyes

The sky falls down when he bangs on the door

And I can't recall anything else than sensing terrible
danger

One more bang and the pieces of the locks are on the
floor

And she would try her best so he can't lay a finger on us
three

18 years have gone by since hiding behind the bed

While he tries to strangle her for how come she dares
answer back

And now he doesn't even recall what he said

Why can't I accept this as the end of the story never
began

<u>Biggest bouquet</u>

He swears on his lawless lands

And for three kids, here comes the taboo

Laid me down and it all ever he comes to when talks about me

Talking through a million little stars

But he painted me blue ignominy

Talked about her with empathy that maybe I couldn't ever afford

Every other syllable wrecks us farther apart

But I'm the one who messed with the harmony

And maybe wanting me to leave is the greatest thing he's done for me

Holds memories

She says your views would be the death of your
happiness

While my eyes reflect the same trajectory of her
shadows,

She hits the younger cause he reflects the trajectory of
his shadow

The windows are tinted red even before life could come
rushing in

She looks for timeless things at an antique shop

And you'd bet she kills and heals at the same time

She was robbed of him before he even came back

Labelled as such a useless thing with her hand studded
with a ring

It's such a useless sin.

The most haunted little man

Two more stabs and while I die screaming,

a million miles away I hope your colourless eyes make

out your blood stained hands

Oh, the most beloved daughter and holy son's protector

make sure to lay them in barren land

So this is the tale of the most haunted little man.

Acknowledgement

+

Firstly, I would like to thank the people without whom this book wouldn't be what it is: Vanshita Jaiswani, Prabhpreet Singh, Prarabdha Singh,VN.Yash Vardhan and milamiart. Without their support and constant help, this wouldn't even be possible.

I would also like to thank the people without whom I wouldn't even be here, my family and the friends I made along the way.

As my brother likes to say, "I like to kick shit." As weird as it sounds, I hope I kicked shit with this one, and thank you to everyone who made it till here; it means the whole world to me.

While concluding, I would like to mention the writings are not connected to my personal life in any way.

Thank You